Overcome Trauma

Reclaiming Your Power and Finding Healing After Trauma

Olivia M. Johnson

Overcome Trauma: Reclaiming Your Power and Finding Healing After Trauma

Published by: Olivia M. Johnson - OMJ Publishing

Address: Phase 6 Block 13 Bahayan Subdivision Luinab, Iligan City Lanao del Norte Philippines 9200

Table of Contents

1 - Introduction..1

2 - Understanding Trauma: Causes, Types, and Symptoms
....3

3 - How Trauma Affects the Brain and Body.......................7

4 - Coping Strategies and Their Limitations......................11

5 - The Importance of Seeking Professional Help............14

6 - Dealing with Shame and Guilt....................................17

7 - Letting Go of Self-Blame and Forgiving Yourself.........21

8 - Developing a Support System.....................................25

9 - The Role of Faith and Spirituality in Healing................28

10 - Mindfulness and Meditation Techniques for Trauma
Survivors...32

11 - Art Therapy and Other Creative Approaches............37

12 - Cognitive Behavioral Therapy for Trauma.................42

13 - Exposure Therapy and Desensitization.....................47

14 - EMDR: Eye Movement Desensitization and Repro-
cessing..52

15 - Medication for PTSD and Other Trauma-Related Dis-
orders..56

16 - Finding a Therapist Who Specializes in Trauma........59

17 - The Challenges of Trust and Intimacy After Trauma..62

18 - Rebuilding Relationships with Family and Friends.....67

19 - Setting Boundaries and Learning to Say No..............71

20 - Building Self-Esteem and Self-Compassion..............74

21 - Identifying Triggers and Developing Coping Skills.....78

22 - Expressing Emotions Safely and Effectively..............83

23 - Resolving Trauma-Related Nightmares and Flash-
backs..87

24 - Overcoming Avoidance and Isolation.......................91

25 - Finding Purpose and Meaning After Trauma.............95

26 - Recognizing and Addressing Secondary Trauma......99

27 - Trauma in Children: How to Help and Support.........103

28 - Trauma in the Workplace: Tips for Employers and Em-
ployees...108

29 - Trauma and Addiction: Breaking the Cycle.............113

30 - Trauma and the Criminal Justice System..................117
31 - Moving Forward: Creating a New Narrative and Embracing Life...121
Thank You...125
Disclaimer..126

1 - Introduction

Trauma is a deeply painful and overwhelming experience that can leave us feeling helpless and powerless. It can shatter our sense of safety and security, and leave us struggling with a range of physical, emotional, and psychological symptoms. But despite the challenges of trauma, healing and recovery are possible.

In "Overcome Trauma: Reclaiming Your Power and Finding Healing After Trauma," we offer a comprehensive guide to navigating the complex and often confusing terrain of trauma recovery. Drawing on the latest research in trauma therapy, as well as our own experiences working with trauma survivors, we offer practical tools and strategies for coping with symptoms, rebuilding relationships, and finding meaning and purpose after trauma.

Our goal in writing this book is to provide a roadmap for healing and growth that is grounded in compassion, understanding, and hope. We recognize that healing from trauma is a complex and ongoing process, and that there is no one-size-fits-all solution. That's why we offer a range of evidence-based therapies and approaches, as well as insights from our own personal and professional journeys.

1 - INTRODUCTION

Whether you are a trauma survivor, a loved one of someone who has experienced trauma, or a therapist working with trauma clients, we hope that "Overcome Trauma" will be a valuable resource on your journey towards healing and wholeness. We believe that by reclaiming your power and finding healing after trauma, you can create a brighter future for yourself and those around you.

2 - Understanding Trauma: Causes, Types, and Symptoms

Trauma is a deeply distressing experience that overwhelms our ability to cope and leaves a lasting impact on our physical, emotional, and psychological well-being. In this chapter, we will explore the causes, types, and symptoms of trauma, and offer insights into how trauma affects our lives.

Causes of Trauma

Trauma can be caused by a wide range of experiences, including:

- Physical or sexual abuse

- Domestic violence

- Natural disasters

- Accidents

- Military combat

- Witnessing violence or death

- Medical procedures

- Neglect or abandonment

- Bullying

- Discrimination or harassment

These experiences can be single or multiple, and can occur at any stage of life. What may be traumatic for one person may not be traumatic for another, as everyone's experiences and reactions are unique.

Types of Trauma

Trauma can be classified into three main types: acute, chronic, and complex.

Acute trauma refers to a single, sudden event that has a significant impact on our lives. Examples of acute trauma include a car accident, a natural disaster, or an assault.

Chronic trauma refers to ongoing, repeated exposure to stressors that leave a lasting impact on our lives. Examples of chronic trauma include domestic violence, ongoing harassment, or living in poverty.

Complex trauma refers to the experience of multiple traumatic events, often occurring in childhood or early adolescence, that are prolonged and interfere with normal development. Examples of complex trauma include physical or sexual abuse, neglect, or living in a war zone.

Symptoms of Trauma

Trauma can have a range of physical, emotional, and psychological symptoms, including:

- Physical symptoms: headaches, muscle tension, fatigue, sleep disturbances, and gastrointestinal problems.

- Emotional symptoms: fear, anxiety, anger, guilt, shame, sadness, and feeling emotionally numb or disconnected.

- Psychological symptoms: flashbacks, nightmares, intrusive thoughts, dissociation, hypervigilance, and difficulty concentrating or making decisions.

2 - UNDERSTANDING TRAUMA: CAUSES, TYPES, AND SYMPTOMS

These symptoms can interfere with our ability to function in our daily lives, affecting our work, relationships, and overall well-being.

In conclusion, understanding the causes, types, and symptoms of trauma is an important first step in the journey towards healing and recovery. By recognizing the impact of trauma on our lives, we can begin to take steps to manage symptoms, develop coping strategies, and seek professional help when needed.

3 - How Trauma Affects the Brain and Body

Trauma can have a profound impact on our brain and body, affecting our thoughts, emotions, and behaviors. In this chapter, we will explore how trauma affects the brain and body, and offer insights into how understanding these effects can aid in the process of healing and recovery.

The Brain's Response to Trauma

When we experience trauma, our brain's stress response system is activated, releasing a flood of hormones that prepare our body for action. This response is known as the "fight or flight" response, and is designed to help us respond to threats and stay safe.

However, when the trauma is overwhelming or prolonged, the stress response can become dysregulated, leading to chronic activation of the stress response system. This can result in a range of changes in the brain, including:

- Changes in the hippocampus: the hippocampus is a part of the brain that is involved in memory formation and regulation. Trauma can lead to changes in the hippocampus, making it more difficult to regulate emotions and recall memories accurately.

- Changes in the amygdala: the amygdala is a part of the brain that is involved in the processing of emotions, particularly fear and anxiety. Trauma can lead to an overactive amygdala, resulting in heightened emotional responses and difficulty regulating emotions.

- Changes in the prefrontal cortex: the prefrontal cortex is a part of the brain that is involved in decision-making, impulse control, and emotional regulation. Trauma can lead to changes in the prefrontal cortex, resulting in difficulty with executive function, such as decision-making and problem-solving.

The Body's Response to Trauma

Trauma can also have a range of effects on the body, including:

- Changes in the autonomic nervous system: the autonomic nervous system is responsible for regulating our bodily functions, such as heart rate, breathing, and digestion. Trauma can lead to dysregulation of the autonomic nervous system, resulting in physical symptoms such as rapid heartbeat, sweating, and nausea.

- Changes in the immune system: trauma can lead to changes in the immune system, making us more vulnerable to illness and infection.

- Changes in the endocrine system: trauma can also lead to changes in the endocrine system, resulting in disruptions to the production and regulation of hormones, which can lead to a range of physical and emotional symptoms.

Healing from Trauma

Understanding how trauma affects the brain and body can be an important step in the process of healing and recovery. By recognizing the ways in which trauma has impacted our thoughts, emotions, and behaviors, we can begin to develop strategies for managing symptoms and building resilience.

Therapies such as cognitive-behavioral therapy, EMDR,

and somatic therapy can help to rewire the brain's response to trauma and address the physical and emotional effects of trauma on the body. Additionally, self-care practices such as mindfulness, exercise, and healthy eating can also be beneficial in the healing process.

In conclusion, trauma can have a profound impact on the brain and body, but understanding these effects can be a powerful tool in the process of healing and recovery. By seeking professional help, developing coping strategies, and engaging in self-care practices, it is possible to reclaim our power and find healing after trauma.

4 - Coping Strategies and Their Limitations

After experiencing trauma, it can be challenging to cope with the physical, emotional, and psychological effects that often follow. In this chapter, we will explore a variety of coping strategies that can be helpful in managing the impact of trauma on our lives, as well as their limitations.

Coping Strategies for Trauma

1. Mindfulness practices: Mindfulness practices such as meditation, deep breathing exercises, and yoga can be helpful in managing the physical symptoms of trauma, such as anxiety and hyperarousal.

2. Social support: Connecting with supportive friends and family members, or joining a support group, can provide a safe and understanding space to share experiences and emotions.

3. Creative expression: Engaging in creative activities such as painting, writing, or music can provide a therapeutic outlet for emotions and help to process traumatic experiences.

4 - COPING STRATEGIES AND THEIR LIMITATIONS

4. Cognitive-behavioral techniques: Techniques such as cognitive restructuring and exposure therapy can help to reframe negative thoughts and emotions related to trauma.

5. Somatic therapy: Somatic therapy approaches such as sensorimotor psychotherapy and somatic experiencing focus on the physical experience of trauma, helping individuals to release stored trauma energy from the body.

Limitations of Coping Strategies

While coping strategies can be helpful in managing the symptoms of trauma, it is important to recognize their limitations. Some limitations include:

1. Coping strategies do not address the root cause of trauma: While coping strategies can help to manage symptoms, they do not address the underlying causes of trauma. To fully heal from trauma, it is often necessary to seek professional help to process and integrate traumatic experiences.

2. Coping strategies may be temporary: Coping

strategies can provide temporary relief from symptoms, but may not provide lasting change. Long-term healing often requires a more comprehensive approach that addresses the root causes of trauma and provides ongoing support.

3. Coping strategies may not be effective for everyone: Coping strategies are not one-size-fits-all and may not be effective for everyone. It is important to explore a variety of strategies and work with a mental health professional to determine which strategies are most helpful for individual needs.

In conclusion, coping strategies can be helpful in managing the symptoms of trauma, but it is important to recognize their limitations. Seeking professional help, addressing the root causes of trauma, and building a support system are essential components of a comprehensive approach to healing and recovery.

5 - The Importance of Seeking Professional Help

While coping strategies can be helpful in managing the symptoms of trauma, seeking professional help is often necessary for long-term healing and recovery. In this chapter, we will explore the importance of seeking professional help and the different types of professionals who can provide support.

Why Seek Professional Help?

1. Trauma can be complex: Trauma can impact individuals in a variety of ways, and the healing process can be complex. Mental health professionals are trained to understand the different ways trauma can impact individuals and provide personalized support.

2. Professional help can address the root cause of trauma: Professional help can provide a safe and supportive space to explore and process traumatic experiences, which can lead to long-term healing and recovery.

3. Professionals can provide evidence-based treatment:

5 - THE IMPORTANCE OF SEEKING PROFESSIONAL HELP

Mental health professionals can provide evidence-based treatments such as cognitive-behavioral therapy, eye movement desensitization and reprocessing (EMDR), and somatic therapy, which have been shown to be effective in treating trauma.

Types of Professionals Who Can Provide Support

1. Therapists: Licensed therapists, such as psychologists, social workers, and counselors, can provide a variety of therapeutic approaches to help individuals heal from trauma.

2. Psychiatrists: Psychiatrists are medical doctors who specialize in mental health and can provide medication management for individuals with trauma-related disorders.

3. Trauma specialists: Some mental health professionals specialize in trauma and can provide specialized treatment such as EMDR, somatic therapy, and other evidence-based approaches.

4. Support groups: Support groups, led by trained facilit-

ators, can provide a supportive community of individuals who have experienced trauma.

5. Crisis hotlines: Crisis hotlines can provide immediate support for individuals experiencing acute distress related to trauma.

In conclusion, seeking professional help is essential for long-term healing and recovery from trauma. Mental health professionals can provide personalized support, evidence-based treatment, and a safe and supportive space to explore and process traumatic experiences. There are a variety of professionals and resources available to individuals seeking help, and it is important to find a support system that works for individual needs.

6 - Dealing with Shame and Guilt

Shame and guilt are two powerful emotions that can have a significant impact on our lives. They are often intertwined, but they are distinct in their experience and manifestation. Shame is the feeling that we are fundamentally flawed, inadequate, or unworthy. Guilt is the feeling of remorse or regret over something we have done or failed to do. Both emotions can be incredibly difficult to deal with, but there are steps we can take to manage them.

Identify the Source of Shame and Guilt

The first step in dealing with shame and guilt is to identify their source. Sometimes, shame and guilt can be caused by external factors, such as societal or cultural norms. For example, if you were raised in a family or community that placed a high value on academic achievement, you may feel shame if you struggle in school. If you were raised in a culture that values stoicism and emotional restraint, you may feel guilt for expressing your emotions openly.

Other times, shame and guilt can be caused by internal factors, such as negative self-talk or unrealistic expectations. For example, if you have a tendency to compare yourself to others and feel that you always fall short, you may experience shame. If you have a perfectionist streak and hold yourself to impossibly high standards, you may feel guilty when you inevitably fall short.

Challenge Negative Self-Talk

Once you have identified the source of your shame and guilt, it's important to challenge any negative self-talk that may be exacerbating these emotions. Negative self-talk can take many forms, from harsh self-criticism to a constant stream of self-doubt. To combat this, try to reframe negative thoughts in a more positive light. For example, if you find yourself thinking, "I'm such a failure," try to reframe that thought by saying, "I may have made a mistake, but that doesn't make me a failure."

Practice Self-Compassion

Another way to deal with shame and guilt is to practice self-compassion. Self-compassion involves treating yourself with the same kindness, care, and understanding that you would offer to a close friend. This means acknowledging your flaws and mistakes without judgment and accepting yourself as you are. It can also involve giving yourself permission to make mistakes and recognizing that failure is a natural part of the learning process.

Make Amends

If your guilt is related to something you have done or failed to do, it's important to take steps to make amends. This may involve apologizing to someone you have hurt, taking responsibility for your actions, or making a concrete effort to right your wrongs. Making amends can help to alleviate feelings of guilt and restore your sense of integrity and self-worth.

Seek Support

Finally, it's important to seek support when dealing with shame and guilt. This may involve talking to a trusted friend or family member, seeking counseling or therapy, or joining a support group. Sharing your experiences with others can help to normalize your feelings and provide you with the support and validation you need to move forward.

In conclusion, dealing with shame and guilt can be challenging, but it's important to remember that these emotions are a normal part of the human experience. By identifying the source of your shame and guilt, challenging negative self-talk, practicing self-compassion, making amends, and seeking support, you can begin to manage these emotions and move towards a healthier, more fulfilling life.

7 - Letting Go of Self-Blame and For-giving Yourself

Letting go of self-blame and forgiving yourself can be a difficult and sometimes painful process, but it is an essential step towards healing and moving forward. When we hold onto feelings of self-blame and guilt, we can become trapped in a cycle of negativity that prevents us from living our lives to the fullest. Here are some steps you can take to let go of self-blame and forgive yourself.

Acknowledge Your Mistakes

The first step in letting go of self-blame and forgiving yourself is to acknowledge your mistakes. This can be a painful process, as it requires us to confront the ways in which we have hurt ourselves or others. However, acknowledging our mistakes is an essential step towards healing and growth. It allows us to take responsibility for our actions and begin to move forward.

Practice Self-Compassion

Once you have acknowledged your mistakes, it's important to practice self-compassion. Self-compassion involves treating yourself with kindness, understanding, and accept-ance, just as you would treat a close friend. It means acknowledging that you are human and that everyone makes mistakes. It also means recognizing that beating yourself up over past mistakes is not productive or helpful.

Identify the Source of Self-Blame

To let go of self-blame, it's important to identify the source of those feelings. Self-blame can be caused by many things, including unrealistic expectations, negative self-talk, or past traumas. By identifying the source of your self-blame, you can begin to challenge those negative beliefs and move towards a more positive outlook.

Challenge Negative Self-Talk

Negative self-talk can be a major contributor to feelings of self-blame and guilt. To combat this, try to reframe negative thoughts in a more positive light. For example, if you find yourself thinking, "I'm such a failure," try to reframe that thought by saying, "I may have made a mistake, but that doesn't make me a failure."

7 - LETTING GO OF SELF-BLAME AND FORGIVING YOURSELF

Make Amends

If your self-blame is related to something you have done or failed to do, it's important to take steps to make amends. This may involve apologizing to someone you have hurt, taking responsibility for your actions, or making a concrete effort to right your wrongs. Making amends can help to alleviate feelings of guilt and restore your sense of integrity and self-worth.

Practice Forgiveness

Finally, to let go of self-blame, it's important to practice forgiveness. This means forgiving yourself for past mistakes and letting go of any lingering feelings of guilt or shame. Forgiveness can be a difficult process, but it is essential for our emotional well-being. It allows us to move forward with a sense of peace and acceptance, rather than being weighed down by past mistakes.

In conclusion, letting go of self-blame and forgiving yourself is an important step towards healing and growth. By acknowledging your mistakes, practicing self-compassion, identifying the source of self-blame, challenging negative self-talk, making amends, and practicing forgiveness, you can begin to let go of the past and move towards a more positive and fulfilling future. Remember, you are human, and everyone makes mistakes. The important thing is to learn from those mistakes and use them as an opportunity for growth and self-improvement.

8 - Developing a Support System

Developing a support system is a critical component of healing and recovery after experiencing trauma. Trauma can leave you feeling isolated, overwhelmed, and powerless, but having a network of supportive people can help you regain a sense of control and create a safe space for processing your emotions. Here are some tips for developing a strong support system after trauma.

Identify Your Needs

The first step in developing a support system is to identify your needs. This may include emotional support, practical assistance with day-to-day tasks, or guidance and advice on how to navigate the healing process. Take some time to reflect on what you need most and prioritize those needs as you seek out support.

Reach Out to Trusted Individuals

Identify people in your life who you trust and feel comfortable opening up to about your trauma. This may include family members, friends, or mental health professionals. Reach out to these individuals and let them know what you are going through. Be clear about what you need from them and ask for their support. Remember, it's okay to set boundaries and communicate your needs clearly.

Join a Support Group

Support groups can be a valuable resource for those who have experienced trauma. They provide a safe space for people to share their experiences, learn from others, and offer mutual support. Look for support groups in your community or online that focus on trauma recovery. Consider joining a group that is tailored to your specific experiences, such as a group for survivors of sexual assault or veterans.

Seek Professional Help

Trauma can have a lasting impact on your mental health, and seeking professional help is often an important part of the healing process. A mental health professional can help you process your trauma, develop coping strategies, and provide ongoing support. Consider working with a therapist who has experience working with trauma survivors.

Engage in Self-Care

Developing a support system is not just about reaching out

to others; it's also about taking care of yourself. Engage in activities that promote self-care, such as exercise, meditation, or spending time in nature. Make sure to prioritize your physical and emotional well-being as you navigate the healing process.

In conclusion, developing a support system is an essential part of healing and recovery after experiencing trauma. By identifying your needs, reaching out to trusted individuals, joining a support group, seeking professional help, and engaging in self-care, you can create a strong network of support that will help you reclaim your power and find healing after trauma. Remember, healing is a journey, and it's okay to reach out for help and support as you navigate the ups and downs of the healing process.

9 - The Role of Faith and Spirituality in Healing

Faith and spirituality can play a significant role in the healing process after trauma. For many people, a strong sense of faith or connection to a higher power can provide comfort, hope, and a sense of meaning and purpose. In this chapter, we will explore the role of faith and spirituality in healing after trauma.

Faith and Coping

Research has shown that faith and spirituality can be powerful coping mechanisms in the face of trauma. For example, studies have found that individuals who identify as religious or spiritual are more likely to use positive coping strategies, such as seeking social support and engaging in self-care, compared to those who do not identify as religious or spiritual.

For many people, faith provides a framework for understanding their experiences and finding meaning and purpose in the midst of suffering. Belief in a higher power can provide comfort and reassurance during times of uncertainty and distress, and can help individuals feel less alone in their struggles.

Spiritual Practices for Healing

There are a variety of spiritual practices that can support healing after trauma. For example:

- Prayer: Many people find comfort and strength through prayer, which can provide a sense of connection to a higher power and a space to express their emotions and needs.

- Meditation: Meditation can help reduce anxiety and stress and improve emotional regulation. Mindfulness meditation, in particular, has been shown to be an effective intervention for trauma-related symptoms.

- Rituals and ceremonies: Rituals and ceremonies, such as lighting candles or performing a ritual of gratitude, can provide a sense of structure and meaning during times of trauma and loss.

- Connection with a spiritual community: For many people, a strong sense of community and connection with others who share their faith or spirituality can provide a sense of belonging and support.

Challenges of Faith and Spirituality in Healing

While faith and spirituality can be powerful tools for healing after trauma, they can also present challenges. For example, individuals who have experienced trauma may struggle with feelings of anger or betrayal towards a higher power or struggle to find meaning in their experiences. Additionally, some individuals may have experienced trauma in the context of a religious or spiritual community, which can lead to feelings of mistrust or disconnection.

It's important to acknowledge that there is no one-size-fits-all approach to integrating faith and spirituality into the healing process. For some, faith and spirituality may be a central part of their healing journey, while for others, it may not resonate at all. It's important to explore what works for you and to approach faith and spirituality with curiosity and openness.

Conclusion

9 - THE ROLE OF FAITH AND SPIRITUALITY IN HEALING

In conclusion, faith and spirituality can play an important role in the healing process after trauma. For many, a strong sense of faith or connection to a higher power can provide comfort, hope, and a sense of meaning and purpose. However, it's important to acknowledge that faith and spirituality can also present challenges and that there is no one-size-fits-all approach to integrating these practices into the healing process. By exploring what works for you and approaching faith and spirituality with curiosity and openness, you can find a path to healing that feels authentic and meaningful.

10 - Mindfulness and Meditation Techniques for Trauma Survivors

Trauma survivors often experience intense emotions and intrusive thoughts that can be overwhelming and difficult to manage. Mindfulness and meditation techniques can be powerful tools for trauma survivors to develop self-awareness, reduce anxiety and stress, and improve emotional regulation. In this chapter, we will explore mindfulness and meditation techniques for trauma survivors.

What is Mindfulness?

Mindfulness is the practice of being fully present and engaged in the current moment, without judgment or distraction. It involves cultivating a non-judgmental awareness of one's thoughts, feelings, and physical sensations. Mindfulness can help trauma survivors develop a sense of control over their thoughts and emotions and reduce their reactivity to triggers.

Meditation Techniques for Trauma Survivors

1. Body Scan Meditation: In body scan meditation, you focus your attention on each part of your body, noti-

cing physical sensations without judgment. This can help you become more aware of your body and identify areas of tension or discomfort that may be related to trauma.

2. Loving-Kindness Meditation: Loving-kindness meditation involves generating feelings of warmth and compassion towards oneself and others. This can help trauma survivors cultivate a sense of self-compassion and improve their relationships with others.

3. Mindful Breathing: Mindful breathing involves focusing your attention on your breath, noticing the sensation of the air moving in and out of your body. This can help you become more grounded and present in the moment.

4. Visualization: Visualization involves creating mental images that evoke feelings of calm or safety. This can help trauma survivors feel more relaxed and centered.

5. Yoga: Yoga combines physical movement with mindfulness and breathing techniques. Practicing yoga

can help trauma survivors release tension and become more aware of their body.

Benefits of Mindfulness and Meditation for Trauma Survivors

- Reducing anxiety and stress: Mindfulness and meditation can help trauma survivors develop a sense of control over their thoughts and emotions, reducing feelings of anxiety and stress.

- Improving emotional regulation: Mindfulness and meditation can help trauma survivors develop emotional regulation skills, allowing them to better manage intense emotions and reduce reactivity to triggers.

- Improving sleep: Trauma survivors often struggle with sleep disturbances. Mindfulness and meditation can help improve sleep quality and reduce insomnia.

- Enhancing self-awareness: Mindfulness and meditation can help trauma survivors become more aware of their thoughts, feelings, and physical sensations, allowing them to better understand their experiences and needs.

- Developing self-compassion: Mindfulness and meditation can help trauma survivors cultivate self-compassion, reducing feelings of shame and self-blame.

Challenges of Mindfulness and Meditation for Trauma Survivors

While mindfulness and meditation can be powerful tools for trauma survivors, they can also present challenges. For example, trauma survivors may find it difficult to focus on their breath or body sensations due to feelings of anxiety or dissociation. Additionally, trauma survivors may experience intense emotions during mindfulness or meditation practice, which can be overwhelming.

It's important for trauma survivors to approach mindfulness and meditation with self-compassion and to seek support from a therapist or other professional if needed. Additionally, trauma survivors may find it helpful to start with shorter meditation sessions and gradually increase the length as they become more comfortable with the practice.

10 - MINDFULNESS AND MEDITATION TECHNIQUES FOR TRAUMA SURVIVORS

Conclusion

In conclusion, mindfulness and meditation techniques can be powerful tools for trauma survivors to develop self-awareness, reduce anxiety and stress, and improve emotional regulation. By incorporating mindfulness and meditation into their daily routine, trauma survivors can develop a sense of control over their thoughts and emotions and improve their overall well-being. However, it's important for trauma survivors to approach these practices with self-compassion and to seek support from a therapist or other professional if needed.

11 - Art Therapy and Other Creative Approaches

Art therapy and other creative approaches can be effective tools for trauma survivors to process their experiences and emotions, express themselves, and promote healing. In this chapter, we will explore art therapy and other creative approaches for trauma survivors.

What is Art Therapy?

Art therapy is a form of therapy that uses creative expression to help individuals explore their emotions and experiences. It can involve a variety of art forms, such as drawing, painting, sculpting, and collage. The art therapist provides a safe and supportive environment for the individual to create and process their artwork, using the artwork as a tool for communication and reflection.

Other Creative Approaches for Trauma Survivors

1. Writing: Writing can be a powerful tool for trauma survivors to express themselves and process their experiences. Writing can take many forms, such as journaling, poetry, and fiction.

2. Music: Music can be a powerful tool for trauma survivors to express themselves and regulate their emotions. Playing an instrument, singing, or listening to
music can all be effective ways to use music for healing.

3. Dance: Dance can be a powerful tool for trauma survivors to connect with their bodies and express themselves. Dancing can help release tension and promote relaxation.

4. Drama: Drama can be a powerful tool for trauma survivors to explore their emotions and experiences in a
safe and supportive environment. Drama therapy can
involve role-playing, improvisation, and other techniques to help individuals process their experiences.

Benefits of Art Therapy and Creative Approaches for Trauma Survivors

- Promoting emotional expression: Art therapy and creative approaches provide a safe and supportive environment for trauma survivors to express their emotions and experiences.

- Enhancing self-awareness: Art therapy and creative approaches can help trauma survivors become more aware of their thoughts, feelings, and physical sensations, allowing them to better understand their experiences and needs.

- Improving emotional regulation: Art therapy and creative approaches can help trauma survivors develop emotional regulation skills, allowing them to better manage intense emotions and reduce reactivity to triggers.

- Increasing sense of control: Art therapy and creative approaches can help trauma survivors develop a sense of control over their experiences, allowing them to make choices and decisions about their artwork and creative expression.

Challenges of Art Therapy and Creative Approaches for Trauma Survivors

While art therapy and creative approaches can be effective tools for trauma survivors, they can also present challenges. For example, trauma survivors may find it difficult to express themselves through art or may experience intense emotions during the creative process. Additionally, trauma survivors may have difficulty finding a safe and supportive environment for their creative expression.

It's important for trauma survivors to approach art therapy and creative approaches with self-compassion and to seek support from a therapist or other professional if needed. Additionally, trauma survivors may find it helpful to start with simple art projects or creative exercises and gradually increase the complexity as they become more comfortable with the process.

Conclusion

In conclusion, art therapy and other creative approaches can be effective tools for trauma survivors to process their experiences and emotions, express themselves, and promote healing. By incorporating art therapy and other creative approaches into their healing journey, trauma survivors can develop a sense of control over their experiences, improve their emotional regulation skills, and enhance their overall well-being. However, it's important for trauma survivors to approach these approaches with self-compassion and to seek support from a therapist or other professional if needed.

12 - Cognitive Behavioral Therapy for Trauma

Cognitive-behavioral therapy (CBT) is a form of psychotherapy that has been shown to be effective in treating trauma-related disorders, such as post-traumatic stress disorder (PTSD), in both adults and children. CBT focuses on the relationship between thoughts, emotions, and behaviors and aims to help individuals develop new, more adaptive ways of thinking and behaving.

In this chapter, we will explore the key principles of CBT and how they can be applied in the treatment of trauma-related disorders.

Principles of CBT for Trauma

1. Education: CBT for trauma typically begins with psychoeducation about trauma and its effects on the brain and body. This education may cover topics such as the fight or flight response, the role of avoidance in PTSD, and common symptoms of trauma.

2. Exposure: Exposure is a key component of CBT for trauma. This involves gradually exposing the indi-

vidual to the traumatic event or a reminder of the traumatic event in a safe and controlled environment. The goal of exposure therapy is to help the individual learn that they can tolerate the emotions and sensations associated with the trauma without being overwhelmed.

3. Cognitive restructuring: CBT for trauma often involves cognitive restructuring, which involves identifying and challenging negative or distorted thoughts related to the traumatic event. The therapist may use techniques such as thought records or cognitive restructuring worksheets to help the individual identify and challenge these thoughts.

4. Behavioral activation: Behavioral activation is another key component of CBT for trauma. This involves engaging in activities that the individual has been avoiding due to their trauma-related symptoms. By engaging in enjoyable activities, the individual can increase positive emotions and decrease avoidance behaviors.

5. Relaxation techniques: CBT for trauma may also in-

volve teaching the individual relaxation techniques, such as deep breathing or progressive muscle relaxation. These techniques can help the individual manage anxiety and other symptoms related to trauma.

Benefits of CBT for Trauma

Research has shown that CBT can be an effective treatment for trauma-related disorders, such as PTSD. Some of the benefits of CBT for trauma include:

1. Improved symptoms: CBT has been shown to reduce symptoms of trauma-related disorders, such as intrusive thoughts, avoidance behaviors, and hyperarousal.

2. Increased coping skills: CBT can help individuals develop coping skills to manage symptoms related to trauma, such as anxiety and anger.

3. Improved quality of life: By reducing symptoms and improving coping skills, CBT can improve an individual's overall quality of life.

4. Long-lasting effects: Research has shown that the

benefits of CBT for trauma can be long-lasting, even after treatment has ended.

Challenges of CBT for Trauma

While CBT can be an effective treatment for trauma-related disorders, it can also present challenges. Some of the challenges of CBT for trauma include:

1. Resistance to exposure: Exposure therapy can be challenging for individuals with trauma-related disorders, as it involves confronting the traumatic event or a reminder of the traumatic event.

2. Time commitment: CBT for trauma typically involves weekly sessions over a period of several months. This can be a significant time commitment for some individuals.

3. Need for a trained therapist: CBT for trauma should be conducted by a therapist who has specialized training in trauma treatment. This can make it difficult for individuals to access this type of treatment in some areas.

Conclusion

In conclusion, CBT is a highly effective treatment for trauma-related disorders, such as PTSD. By helping individuals develop coping skills, challenging negative thoughts, and gradually exposing them to the traumatic event, CBT can reduce symptoms and improve an individual's quality of life. However, it's important for individuals to work with a trained therapist who has experience in trauma treatment and to approach treatment with patience and self-compassion.

13 - Exposure Therapy and Desensitization

Exposure therapy and desensitization are two techniques used in the treatment of trauma-related disorders, such as post-traumatic stress disorder (PTSD). In this chapter, we will explore the principles of exposure therapy and desensitization and how they can be used to help individuals overcome the effects of trauma.

Principles of Exposure Therapy and Desensitization

Exposure therapy and desensitization are based on the principle of habituation. Habituation occurs when an individual is exposed to a fear-provoking stimulus repeatedly until the fear response diminishes. In the context of trauma treatment, exposure therapy and desensitization involve gradually exposing the individual to the traumatic event or a reminder of the traumatic event in a safe and controlled environment.

The process of exposure therapy and desensitization typically involves the following steps:

1. Psychoeducation: The therapist provides education

to the individual about trauma and its effects on the brain and body. This education may include information about the fight or flight response, the role of avoidance in PTSD, and common symptoms of trauma.

2. Building coping skills: Before beginning exposure therapy or desensitization, the therapist works with the individual to develop coping skills to manage anxiety and other symptoms related to trauma.

3. Identifying triggers: The therapist helps the individual identify triggers, or situations or reminders that elicit a fear response.

4. Graded exposure: The therapist works with the individual to create a hierarchy of fear-provoking stimuli, starting with the least anxiety-provoking and gradually progressing to more anxiety-provoking stimuli.

5. Exposure: The individual is exposed to the fear-provoking stimuli in a safe and controlled environment. This may involve visualizing the traumatic event, looking at pictures or videos related to the event, or

engaging in real-life situations that are similar to the traumatic event.

6. Desensitization: Over time, the individual becomes desensitized to the fear-provoking stimuli, and the fear response diminishes.

Benefits of Exposure Therapy and Desensitization

Research has shown that exposure therapy and desensitization can be effective treatments for trauma-related disorders, such as PTSD. Some of the benefits of exposure therapy and desensitization include:

1. Reduced symptoms: Exposure therapy and desensitization have been shown to reduce symptoms of trauma-related disorders, such as intrusive thoughts, avoidance behaviors, and hyperarousal.

2. Increased coping skills: Exposure therapy and desensitization can help individuals develop coping skills to manage symptoms related to trauma, such as anxiety and anger.

3. Improved quality of life: By reducing symptoms and

improving coping skills, exposure therapy and de-sensitization can improve an individual's overall quality of life.

4. Long-lasting effects: Research has shown that the benefits of exposure therapy and desensitization can be long-lasting, even after treatment has ended.

Challenges of Exposure Therapy and Desensitization

While exposure therapy and desensitization can be effective treatments for trauma-related disorders, they can also present challenges. Some of the challenges of exposure therapy and desensitization include:

1. Resistance to exposure: Exposure therapy can be challenging for individuals with trauma-related disorders, as it involves confronting the traumatic event or a reminder of the traumatic event.

2. Time commitment: Exposure therapy typically involves weekly sessions over a period of several months. This can be a significant time commitment for some individuals.

3. Need for a trained therapist: Exposure therapy should be conducted by a therapist who has specialized training in trauma treatment. This can make it difficult for individuals to access this type of treatment in some areas.

Conclusion

In conclusion, exposure therapy and desensitization are highly effective treatments for trauma-related disorders, such as PTSD. By gradually exposing the individual to the fear-provoking stimuli in a safe and controlled environment, exposure therapy and desensitization can help individuals overcome their fear and trauma-related symptoms, develop coping skills, and improve their overall quality of life.

While these treatments can present challenges and require a trained therapist, the long-lasting benefits make them worthwhile options for those struggling with trauma. It is important to consult with a mental health professional to determine if exposure therapy and desensitization are appropriate treatments for your individual needs. With the right support and treatment, individuals can overcome trauma and reclaim their power.

14 - EMDR: Eye Movement Desensitization and Reprocessing

Eye Movement Desensitization and Reprocessing (EMDR) is a form of psychotherapy that is designed to help individuals overcome trauma and other distressing life experiences. The approach was developed in the 1980s by psychologist Francine Shapiro, who discovered that eye movements can reduce the intensity of disturbing thoughts and emotions.

EMDR is based on the idea that traumatic experiences can become "stuck" in the brain, causing persistent distress and interfering with daily functioning. The therapy aims to help individuals process the traumatic memories and related emotions in a more adaptive way, allowing them to move forward with their lives.

The EMDR process involves several steps, including:

1. History-taking and assessment: The therapist will gather information about the individual's trauma history and current symptoms to create a treatment plan tailored to their needs.

2. Preparation: The therapist will help the individual de-

velop coping skills and relaxation techniques to use during the EMDR process.

3. Desensitization: The individual will focus on a specific traumatic memory while simultaneously engaging in eye movements or other forms of bilateral stimulation, such as tapping or auditory tones. This process is thought to activate the brain's natural healing processes, allowing the individual to process the memory in a more adaptive way.

4. Installation: The therapist will help the individual strengthen positive beliefs and emotions related to the traumatic memory.

5. Body scan: The individual will focus on physical sensations related to the traumatic memory to ensure that the processing is complete.

6. Closure: The therapist will help the individual return to a state of calmness and relaxation after the processing is complete.

7. Reevaluation: The therapist and individual will assess

the progress made and determine if additional EMDR sessions are needed.

Research has shown that EMDR can be an effective treatment for trauma-related disorders, including post-traumatic stress disorder (PTSD). Studies have also suggested that EMDR may be as effective as other forms of trauma-focused therapy, such as cognitive-behavioral therapy (CBT).

One of the benefits of EMDR is that it can be completed in a relatively short period of time, with some individuals experiencing significant symptom reduction after just a few sessions. EMDR has also been found to be effective for a wide range of trauma types, including combat trauma, childhood abuse, and natural disasters.

It is important to note that EMDR may not be appropriate for everyone, and some individuals may require additional support or a different type of therapy to address their trauma. Additionally, EMDR should only be conducted by a trained therapist who is licensed to practice psychotherapy.

In conclusion, EMDR is a promising therapy option for individuals struggling with trauma-related symptoms. By processing traumatic memories in a safe and controlled environment, individuals can reduce their distress and improve their overall functioning. If you or someone you know is struggling with trauma, it is important to seek the guidance of a mental health professional to determine the best course of treatment.

15 - Medication for PTSD and Other Trauma-Related Disorders

Medication can be an important tool in the treatment of post-traumatic stress disorder (PTSD) and other trauma-related disorders. While medication alone is not typically considered a first-line treatment for PTSD, it may be used in conjunction with therapy and other interventions to help alleviate symptoms and improve overall functioning.

There are several classes of medication that are commonly used to treat PTSD and other trauma-related disorders, including:

1. Selective serotonin reuptake inhibitors (SSRIs): SSRIs are a type of antidepressant that can help alleviate symptoms of depression and anxiety, which are common in individuals with PTSD. Examples of SSRIs include sertraline (Zoloft), fluoxetine (Prozac), and paroxetine (Paxil).

2. Serotonin-norepinephrine reuptake inhibitors (SNRIs): SNRIs are similar to SSRIs in that they help regulate levels of serotonin and norepinephrine, two neurotransmitters that play a role in mood regulation.

Examples of SNRIs include venlafaxine (Effexor) and duloxetine (Cymbalta).

3. Benzodiazepines: Benzodiazepines are a class of medication that can help alleviate anxiety symptoms, but they are typically used on a short-term basis due to the potential for dependence and addiction. Examples of benzodiazepines include clonazepam (Klonopin) and lorazepam (Ativan).

4. Antipsychotics: Antipsychotics are typically used to treat symptoms of psychosis, such as hallucinations and delusions, but they may also be used to alleviate symptoms of PTSD in some individuals. Examples of antipsychotics include risperidone (Risperdal) and quetiapine (Seroquel).

5. Prazosin: Prazosin is a medication that is commonly used to treat high blood pressure, but it has also been found to be effective in reducing nightmares and other sleep disturbances in individuals with PTSD.

While medication can be helpful in reducing symptoms of

15 - MEDICATION FOR PTSD AND OTHER TRAUMA-RE-LATED DISORDERS

PTSD and other trauma-related disorders, it is important to note that it is not a cure for these conditions. Additionally, not all individuals will respond to medication in the same way, and it may take some trial and error to find the right medication and dosage.

It is also important to work closely with a mental health professional when using medication to treat trauma-related disorders. This can help ensure that the medication is being used safely and effectively, and can help monitor for any potential side effects or interactions with other medications.

In conclusion, medication can be a helpful tool in the treatment of PTSD and other trauma-related disorders, but it should be used in conjunction with therapy and other interventions. Working closely with a mental health professional can help ensure that medication is being used safely and effectively, and can help monitor for any potential side effects or interactions with other medications. If you or someone you know is struggling with PTSD or another trauma-related disorder, it is important to seek the guidance of a mental health professional to determine the best course of treatment.

16 - Finding a Therapist Who Specializes in Trauma

Finding a therapist who specializes in trauma can be a daunting task, especially when you are already dealing with the effects of trauma. However, finding the right therapist can be a crucial step in your healing journey.

Trauma can manifest in a variety of ways, such as anxiety, depression, post-traumatic stress disorder (PTSD), and other mental health issues. Therefore, it is important to find a therapist who is trained and experienced in treating trauma.

Here are some tips on how to find a therapist who specializes in trauma:

1. Ask for referrals: The first step in finding a therapist is to ask for referrals from trusted sources, such as your primary care physician, friends, family, or other healthcare providers. They may know of a therapist who specializes in trauma and can provide you with a list of names.

2. Check credentials: Once you have a list of potential

therapists, check their credentials. Look for therapists who are licensed and have experience treating trauma. You can also check their professional affiliations, such as the International Society for Traumatic Stress Studies or the Association for Behavioral and Cognitive Therapies.

3. Research their approach: Different therapists use different approaches when treating trauma. Some may use cognitive-behavioral therapy (CBT), while others may use eye movement desensitization and reprocessing (EMDR). Do some research on the different approaches and see which one resonates with you.

4. Consider the therapist's personality: Finding a therapist who you feel comfortable with is crucial for a successful therapeutic relationship. You may want to schedule an initial consultation to see if you feel comfortable talking to the therapist and if you feel like they understand your needs.

5. Check their availability: Trauma therapy may require more frequent sessions, so it is important to find a

therapist who has availability that fits your schedule. Consider the therapist's office location and their hours of operation.

6. Check their insurance coverage: If you have insurance, check if the therapist is covered by your plan. If you do not have insurance, ask the therapist about their fees and if they offer a sliding scale based on income.

7. Read reviews: Look for reviews of the therapist online. This can give you an idea of other people's experiences with the therapist and their success in treating trauma.

In conclusion, finding a therapist who specializes in trauma requires some research and effort, but it is well worth it for your healing journey. Remember to prioritize finding a therapist who you feel comfortable with and who has experience treating trauma. With the right therapist, you can begin to heal from the effects of trauma and move towards a healthier and happier life.

17 - The Challenges of Trust and Intimacy After Trauma

Trauma can have profound and lasting effects on a person's ability to trust others and develop intimacy in relationships. Whether the trauma stems from physical or emotional abuse, neglect, or a traumatic event, the aftermath can make it challenging to trust others and form intimate connections. In this chapter, we will explore the challenges of trust and intimacy after trauma and some strategies for healing and building healthy relationships.

Trauma and Trust

Trauma can shatter our sense of safety and security, leaving us feeling vulnerable and distrustful of others. When someone experiences trauma, their brain often responds with hyper-vigilance, constantly scanning for potential threats. This can lead to a generalized sense of mistrust, making it challenging to feel safe around others, even in non-threatening situations.

Trust is a fundamental component of healthy relationships, and without it, intimacy and connection are difficult to achieve. Trauma survivors may struggle to trust others due to the betrayal they experienced during their trauma. For example, if someone was physically or emotionally abused by a caregiver, they may struggle to trust anyone in a caregiving role. Similarly, if someone was sexually assaulted by a trusted friend or family member, they may struggle to trust anyone in a close relationship.

Trauma and Intimacy

Intimacy involves sharing oneself vulnerably with another person, both emotionally and physically. Trauma can make it difficult to develop this level of vulnerability and closeness. When someone has experienced trauma, they may have developed coping mechanisms to avoid vulnerability, such as dissociating or numbing their emotions. These coping mechanisms can make it challenging to connect with others emotionally, as they may struggle to identify and express their feelings.

In addition, trauma survivors may experience physical symptoms that make physical intimacy uncomfortable or triggering. For example, someone who experienced sexual trauma may struggle with sexual intimacy or may have physical symptoms such as pain or tension during sexual activity.

Strategies for Healing

Rebuilding trust and intimacy after trauma is a challenging and often lengthy process. However, with support and guidance, it is possible to develop healthy and fulfilling relationships.

Therapy: Trauma-focused therapy can help survivors process their trauma, develop coping mechanisms, and work through trust and intimacy issues. Therapists trained in trauma-focused therapies such as Cognitive Behavioral Therapy (CBT), Eye Movement Desensitization and Reprocessing (EMDR), or Trauma-Focused Cognitive Behavioral Therapy (TF-CBT) can help survivors build skills for coping with trauma triggers, managing emotions, and improving relationships.

Self-care: Practicing self-care is essential for survivors of trauma. Self-care can include activities such as exercise, meditation, yoga, or spending time in nature. It is essential to prioritize self-care and make time for activities that promote relaxation, reduce stress, and enhance well-being.

Communication: Communication is key to building trust and intimacy in relationships. Trauma survivors may struggle to communicate their needs and feelings, making it challenging to establish healthy relationships. Learning to communicate effectively can help survivors express themselves clearly and establish boundaries, which can improve relationships.

Patience and understanding: Healing from trauma takes time, and survivors may need time and space to work through their experiences. It is essential to be patient and understanding, respecting survivors' boundaries and needs. Pushing survivors to move beyond their comfort zone or dismissing their feelings can further damage trust and intimacy.

Conclusion

Trauma can have a profound impact on a person's ability to trust others and develop intimacy in relationships. Rebuilding trust and intimacy after trauma is a challenging process that requires support, patience, and understanding.

17 - THE CHALLENGES OF TRUST AND INTIMACY AFTER TRAUMA

Through therapy, self-care, effective communication, and patience, it is possible to develop healthy and fulfilling relationships after trauma.

18 - Rebuilding Relationships with Family and Friends

Rebuilding Relationships with Family and Friends

Trauma can have a significant impact on our relationships with family and friends. It may cause us to withdraw from social connections or lead to strained relationships with loved ones. However, rebuilding relationships with family and friends is an essential part of the healing process. In this chapter, we will explore some strategies for rebuilding relationships after experiencing trauma.

1. Communicate Openly and Honestly

   Communication is key to rebuilding relationships. It is essential to communicate openly and honestly with loved ones about how trauma has affected us and what we need from them moving forward. This may involve sharing difficult emotions or asking for support in a particular area. Being vulnerable can be challenging, but it can also lead to deeper connections with those we care about.

2. Practice Active Listening

Active listening is a skill that can enhance communication and promote understanding in relationships. It involves giving our full attention to the speaker, asking clarifying questions, and reflecting back what we hear to ensure we understand correctly. This can help us to better understand the perspectives and needs of our loved ones and strengthen our connections.

3. Set Boundaries

Setting boundaries is essential in any healthy relationship. This is especially important after experiencing trauma, as we may need to protect ourselves from triggering situations or people. It is okay to say no or to ask for space when we need it. By setting boundaries, we can take care of ourselves while also maintaining healthy relationships with our loved ones.

4. Seek Professional Help

Sometimes, rebuilding relationships after trauma may require the support of a professional. Therapy can help us to process our emotions and develop coping skills, which can improve our ability to communicate and connect with others. It may also be helpful to attend family therapy sessions, where a therapist can facilitate communication and provide a safe space for all parties to express their needs and concerns.

5. Practice Self-Care

Taking care of ourselves is essential for rebuilding relationships. It is difficult to connect with others when we are feeling overwhelmed or burnt out. Practicing self-care can involve anything from getting enough rest, eating well, exercising, or engaging in activities that bring us joy. When we prioritize our own well-being, we are better able to show up for our loved ones.

Conclusion

Rebuilding relationships after experiencing trauma may be challenging, but it is also a crucial step in the healing process. By communicating openly, practicing active listening, setting boundaries, seeking professional help, and practicing self-care, we can improve our relationships with family and friends and create deeper connections. Remember, healing is a process, and it takes time. Be patient with yourself and others as you navigate this journey.

19 - Setting Boundaries and Learning to Say No

After experiencing trauma, it can be challenging to navigate relationships and set boundaries. Trauma may have left us feeling vulnerable, and we may struggle to trust others or to assert our needs. However, setting boundaries and learning to say no are essential parts of the healing process. In this chapter, we will explore some strategies for setting boundaries and learning to say no after experiencing trauma.

1. Identify Your Boundaries

   The first step in setting boundaries is to identify them. This may involve reflecting on your values, needs, and priorities. Consider what makes you feel uncomfortable or unsafe, and what behaviors or situations you want to avoid. This can help you to establish clear boundaries and communicate them to others.

2. Communicate Your Boundaries

   Once you have identified your boundaries, it is essential to communicate them to others. This can involve expressing your needs, expectations, and limits clearly and assertively. Use "I" statements to describe how you feel, rather than blaming or accusing others. Be specific and direct, and avoid apologizing or justifying your boundaries.

3. Practice Saying No

Learning to say no can be difficult, especially if we have a history of people-pleasing or accommodating others at the expense of our own needs. However, saying no is an essential part of setting boundaries and taking care of ourselves. Practice saying no in low-stakes situations, such as declining invitations or requests that don't align with your boundaries. This can help you to build confidence and assertiveness over time.

4. Seek Support

Setting boundaries and saying no can be challenging, especially if we fear conflict or rejection. It can be helpful to seek support from trusted friends, family, or professionals. This may involve role-playing scenarios or practicing communication strategies with a therapist or coach. Surround yourself with people who respect and support your boundaries and provide encouragement as you practice saying no.

5. Practice Self-Care

Setting boundaries and saying no may feel uncomfortable at first, but it is essential for our well-being. It is okay to prioritize your own needs and take time for self-care, such as taking breaks, engaging in hobbies, or seeking professional help. When we take care of ourselves, we are better able to show up for others and maintain healthy relationships.

Conclusion

Setting boundaries and learning to say no are essential parts of the healing process after experiencing trauma. By identifying our boundaries, communicating them clearly, practicing saying no, seeking support, and practicing self-care, we can take care of ourselves and create healthy relationships with others. Remember, setting boundaries takes time and practice, but it is worth it for our well-being.

20 - Building Self-Esteem and Self-Compassion

Trauma can have a significant impact on our self-esteem and self-worth. It may lead us to feel inadequate, ashamed, or unworthy of love and respect. However, building self-esteem and self-compassion is an essential part of the healing process. In this chapter, we will explore some strategies for building self-esteem and self-compassion after experiencing trauma.

1. Practice Self-Affirmations

Self-affirmations are positive statements that we repeat to ourselves to counter negative self-talk and beliefs. They can help us to reframe our thoughts and focus on our strengths and accomplishments. Choose affirmations that resonate with you and repeat them regularly, such as "I am worthy of love and respect," "I am strong and capable," or "I am deserving of happiness."

2. Challenge Negative Self-Talk

Negative self-talk can be a significant barrier to building self-esteem and self-compassion. It can be challenging to break free from self-criticism and self-blame, especially after experiencing trauma. However, it is possible to challenge negative self-talk by identifying the evidence for and against the negative beliefs. Ask yourself, "Is this thought true? What evidence do I have to support it? What evidence do I have to challenge it?" This can help you to reframe your thoughts and develop more self-compassionate beliefs.

3. Cultivate Self-Compassion

Self-compassion is the practice of treating ourselves with kindness, understanding, and acceptance, especially when we are struggling. It involves acknowledging our emotions and experiences without judgment or self-blame. Cultivating self-compassion can involve practices such as self-care, mindfulness, and self-compassionate language. Treat yourself with the same kindness and compassion you would offer to a friend.

4. Engage in Activities You Enjoy

Engaging in activities that bring us joy and fulfillment can be a powerful way to build self-esteem and self-compassion. This may involve hobbies, creative pursuits, exercise, or spending time with loved ones. When we engage in activities that align with our values and interests, we can feel more confident and self-assured.

5. Seek Professional Help

Sometimes, building self-esteem and self-compassion may require the support of a professional. Therapy can help us to identify and challenge negative beliefs, develop coping skills, and build resilience. It may also be helpful to attend support groups or workshops where we can connect with others who have had similar experiences and share strategies for building self-esteem and self-compassion.

Conclusion

Building self-esteem and self-compassion after experiencing trauma may take time and practice, but it is worth it for our well-being. By practicing self-affirmations, challenging negative self-talk, cultivating self-compassion, engaging in activities we enjoy, and seeking professional help, we can develop a stronger sense of self-worth and self-acceptance. Remember, healing is a process, and it takes time. Be patient with yourself and celebrate your progress along the way.

21 - Identifying Triggers and Developing Coping Skills

Trauma can have a lasting impact on our lives, even long after the event has passed. It can affect the way we think, feel, and behave, and may even lead to the development of post-traumatic stress disorder (PTSD). One of the keys to managing the symptoms of trauma is to identify triggers and develop coping skills. In this chapter, we will explore some strategies for identifying triggers and developing coping skills to help manage the effects of trauma.

1. Identifying Triggers

Triggers are people, places, things, or situations that can bring up memories or feelings associated with the traumatic event. Common triggers include loud noises, crowded places, certain smells or tastes, or specific times of day. Identifying triggers is an essential first step in managing the effects of trauma. Take some time to reflect on situations that cause you to feel anxious, fearful, or overwhelmed. Keep a journal of these triggers and note any patterns or similarities between them.

2. Developing Coping Skills

Coping skills are strategies we use to manage diffi-cult emotions and situations. Developing coping skills can help us to feel more in control and reduce the im-pact of triggers. There are many different coping skills that may be helpful, depending on your prefer-ences and needs. Some common coping skills in-clude:

- Deep breathing: Slow, deep breathing can help to calm the body and reduce anxiety. Practice taking deep breaths in through the nose and out through the mouth.

- Grounding techniques: Grounding techniques involve using your senses to focus on the present moment. For example, you might focus on the feeling of your feet on the ground, the sounds around you, or the smell of a comforting scent.

- Exercise: Exercise can help to release tension and improve mood. Find an activity you enjoy, such as walking, yoga, or swimming.

- Self-care: Taking care of yourself can help to reduce stress and promote relaxation. This might involve taking a bath, reading a book, or listening to music.

- Social support: Connecting with others who understand and support you can be a powerful coping strategy. Consider reaching out to friends, family, or a support group for help.

3. Practice Self-Compassion

Practicing self-compassion involves treating ourselves with kindness and understanding, especially when we are struggling. Trauma can lead to feelings of shame, guilt, or self-blame, which can make it difficult to cope with triggers. However, by practicing self-compassion, we can develop a greater sense of self-acceptance and resilience. Some ways to practice self-compassion include:

- Talking to yourself with kindness and understanding

- Acknowledging your emotions and experiences without judgment

- Practicing self-care and self-nurturing activities

- Setting healthy boundaries and practicing assertiveness

4. Seek Professional Help

If you are struggling to manage the effects of trauma
on your own, it may be helpful to seek professional
help. Therapy can help you to identify triggers, develop coping skills, and work through the emotional
impact of the traumatic event. Your therapist may
also recommend other treatments, such as medication or eye movement desensitization and reprocessing (EMDR), to help manage PTSD symptoms.

Conclusion

Identifying triggers and developing coping skills is an essential part of managing the effects of trauma. By identifying triggers and developing coping skills, you can feel more
in control and reduce the impact of trauma on your life. Remember to be patient with yourself, and celebrate your progress along the way. With time and practice, you can de-

velop a greater sense of resilience and well-being.

22 - Expressing Emotions Safely and Effectively

Trauma can have a profound impact on our emotional well-being, leading to feelings of fear, anger, sadness, and confusion. One of the key challenges of trauma recovery is learning to express these emotions safely and effectively. In this chapter, we will explore some strategies for expressing emotions in a healthy and constructive way.

1. Understand Your Emotions

   The first step in expressing emotions safely and effectively is to understand them. Trauma can lead to complex and overwhelming emotions that can be difficult to navigate. Take some time to identify the emotions you are experiencing and consider the underlying causes. For example, if you are feeling angry, is it because of something that happened recently or is it related to the traumatic event?

2. Practice Mindfulness

   Practicing mindfulness can help you to become more aware of your emotions and how they impact your body and mind. Mindfulness involves focusing on the present moment without judgment or distraction. This can help you to become more attuned to your emotions and develop a greater sense of self-awareness. Consider practicing mindfulness techniques, such as meditation or deep breathing, to help regulate your emotions.

3. Use "I" Statements

When expressing emotions, it is important to use "I" statements instead of "you" statements. "I" statements focus on your feelings and experiences, while "you" statements can be perceived as blaming or confrontational. For example, instead of saying "You always make me feel angry," try saying "I feel angry when this happens." This can help to promote effective communication and reduce the risk of conflict.

4. Practice Active Listening

Effective communication involves not only expressing your own emotions but also listening to others. Practice active listening by focusing on the speaker and asking questions to clarify their message. This can help to promote empathy and understanding and reduce the risk of misunderstandings.

5. Use Writing or Art as a Medium

Writing or art can be a powerful tool for expressing emotions in a safe and constructive way. Consider keeping a journal or creating artwork as a way to process your emotions. This can also help to identify patterns and triggers that may be contributing to your emotional state.

6. Seek Professional Help

If you are struggling to express emotions safely and effectively on your own, it may be helpful to seek professional help. Therapy can provide a safe and supportive environment to explore your emotions and develop healthy coping strategies. Your therapist may also recommend other treatments, such as cognitive-behavioral therapy (CBT), to help manage the emotional impact of trauma.

Conclusion

Expressing emotions safely and effectively is an essential part of trauma recovery. By understanding your emotions, practicing mindfulness, using "I" statements, practicing active listening, using writing or art as a medium, and seeking professional help when needed, you can learn to express your emotions in a healthy and constructive way. Remember to be patient with yourself, and celebrate your progress along the way. With time and practice, you can develop a greater sense of emotional resilience and well-being.

23 - Resolving Trauma-Related Nightmares and Flashbacks

One of the most common and distressing symptoms of trauma is the experience of nightmares and flashbacks. These can be terrifying and overwhelming, and can make it difficult to sleep or focus on daily activities. In this chapter, we will explore some strategies for resolving trauma-related nightmares and flashbacks.

1. Understand Trauma-Related Nightmares and Flashbacks

   The first step in resolving trauma-related nightmares and flashbacks is to understand what they are and why they occur. Trauma-related nightmares and flashbacks are a normal response to traumatic events, and are the brain's way of processing and integrating traumatic experiences. They may be triggered by reminders of the trauma, such as sights, sounds, or smells, or they may occur spontaneously. Understanding this can help to reduce the fear and anxiety associated with nightmares and flashbacks.

2. Develop a Bedtime Routine

Establishing a regular bedtime routine can help to promote relaxation and reduce the risk of nightmares and flashbacks. Consider incorporating activities that promote relaxation, such as taking a warm bath, practicing deep breathing, or listening to calming music. Avoid stimulating activities, such as watching TV or using electronics, before bedtime.

3. Practice Grounding Techniques

Grounding techniques can be helpful in managing flashbacks and staying present in the moment. These techniques involve focusing on the present moment and using the senses to become more aware of your surroundings. For example, you might try focusing on the feeling of your feet on the ground, or taking deep breaths and focusing on the sensation of air entering and leaving your lungs.

4. Create a Safe Space

Creating a safe space can help to reduce the fear and anxiety associated with nightmares and flashbacks. This can be a physical space, such as a comfortable and calming room, or a mental space, such as a visualization of a safe and peaceful environment. Consider practicing this visualization regularly, especially before bedtime or during times of stress.

5. Seek Professional Help

If nightmares and flashbacks are severely impacting your daily life, it may be helpful to seek professional help. Therapy can provide a safe and supportive environment to explore the underlying causes of nightmares and flashbacks, and develop effective coping strategies. Your therapist may also recommend other treatments, such as eye movement desensitization and reprocessing (EMDR) or cognitive-behavioral therapy (CBT), to help manage the impact of trauma-related nightmares and flashbacks.

Conclusion

Resolving trauma-related nightmares and flashbacks can be a challenging process, but with time and practice, it is possible to manage and reduce their impact. By understanding trauma-related nightmares and flashbacks, developing a bedtime routine, practicing grounding techniques, creating a safe space, and seeking professional help when needed, you can begin to take control of your symptoms and work towards a greater sense of well-being. Remember to be patient and compassionate with yourself, and celebrate your progress along the way.

24 - Overcoming Avoidance and Isolation

One of the most common ways that people cope with trauma is by avoiding situations or people that may trigger memories of the traumatic event. While this may provide temporary relief, over time, avoidance can lead to feelings of isolation and detachment from others. In this chapter, we will explore some strategies for overcoming avoidance and isolation and reconnecting with others.

1. Understand the Impact of Avoidance and Isolation

   The first step in overcoming avoidance and isolation is to understand the impact that these behaviors can have on your life. Avoidance can lead to missed opportunities for growth and connection, and can reinforce feelings of fear and anxiety. Isolation can lead to feelings of loneliness and disconnection, and can make it difficult to seek out support from others. By recognizing these negative impacts, you can begin to take steps towards change.

2. Practice Mindfulness

Practicing mindfulness can help to increase aware-ness of avoidance and isolation behaviors, and can provide a pathway towards greater self-awareness and connection with others. Mindfulness involves fo-cusing on the present moment, and observing thoughts and feelings without judgment. By practicing mindfulness regularly, you can become more aware of avoidance and isolation behaviors, and begin to challenge them in a more intentional way.

3. Seek Out Support

Reaching out to others can be difficult when you are experiencing avoidance and isolation, but seeking out support is a crucial step in overcoming these be-haviors. Consider reaching out to friends or family members, or seeking support from a therapist or sup-port group. Having a trusted and supportive person to talk to can help to increase feelings of connection and reduce feelings of isolation.

4. Take Small Steps

Overcoming avoidance and isolation can be a challenging process, and it is important to take small steps towards change. Consider setting small goals for yourself, such as attending a social event or reaching out to a friend for support. Celebrate your successes along the way, and remember that change takes time.

5. Practice Self-Compassion

Finally, it is important to practice self-compassion throughout the process of overcoming avoidance and isolation. Remember that healing from trauma is a process, and that setbacks are a natural part of that process. Be kind and compassionate with yourself, and recognize that you are taking important steps towards healing and growth.

Conclusion

Overcoming avoidance and isolation is a crucial step towards healing from trauma and reconnecting with others. By understanding the impact of avoidance and isolation, practicing mindfulness, seeking out support, taking small steps towards change, and practicing self-compassion, you can begin to break free from these behaviors and move towards a greater sense of well-being. Remember that change takes time, and that seeking support from others is a sign of strength and resilience.

25 - Finding Purpose and Meaning After Trauma

Trauma can shatter our sense of self and leave us feeling lost and without direction. However, it is possible to find purpose and meaning after trauma. In this chapter, we will explore some strategies for finding meaning and purpose in life after experiencing trauma.

1. Reflect on Your Values and Beliefs

   Trauma can challenge our core beliefs and values, and it is important to take the time to reflect on what is truly important to us. Consider what values and beliefs guide your life, and how they have been impacted by your trauma. Reflecting on these values and beliefs can help to clarify what is truly important to you, and can guide your search for purpose and meaning.

2. Explore Your Passions and Interests

   Identifying your passions and interests can be a powerful way to connect with a sense of purpose and meaning in life. Consider what activities bring you joy and fulfillment, and explore ways to integrate these activities into your daily life. Whether it is a hobby or a career path, pursuing your passions can provide a sense of direction and fulfillment.

3. Volunteer or Give Back

Giving back to others can be a meaningful way to find purpose and meaning after trauma. Consider volunteering for a cause that is important to you, or find ways to help others in your community. Not only can this provide a sense of purpose, but it can also provide a sense of connection and community.

4. Connect with Others

Connecting with others who have experienced trauma can provide a sense of purpose and meaning in life. Consider joining a support group or reaching out to others who have experienced similar struggles. Sharing your experiences with others can help to build a sense of community and can provide a sense of purpose in helping others who have gone through similar experiences.

5. Seek Professional Help

Working with a therapist or counselor can be a powerful way to explore your sense of purpose and meaning in life after trauma. A mental health professional can help you to identify your values and passions, and can guide you in finding ways to integrate them into your life. Additionally, therapy can help to address any underlying issues related to trauma that may be impacting your ability to find purpose and meaning.

Conclusion

Finding purpose and meaning after trauma can be a challenging process, but it is possible. By reflecting on your values and beliefs, exploring your passions and interests, volunteering or giving back, connecting with others, and seeking professional help, you can begin to rebuild a sense of purpose and meaning in life. Remember that healing from trauma is a process, and that finding purpose and meaning may take time. However, with persistence and support, it is possible to find a sense of direction and fulfillment after experiencing trauma.

26 - Recognizing and Addressing Secondary Trauma

Trauma doesn't just affect those who directly experience it. It can also impact those who work with or care for individuals who have experienced trauma, such as mental health professionals, first responders, and family members. This is known as secondary trauma, or vicarious trauma. In this chapter, we will explore how to recognize and address secondary trauma.

1. Recognizing Secondary Trauma

The first step in addressing secondary trauma is recognizing its signs and symptoms. Some common signs of secondary trauma include:

- Feeling emotionally exhausted or overwhelmed

- Difficulty sleeping or nightmares

- Avoiding situations or clients that trigger memories of trauma

- Becoming emotionally numb or detached from clients or loved ones

- Feeling irritable or angry

- Experiencing physical symptoms, such as headaches or stomachaches

1. If you notice any of these symptoms in yourself or a colleague, it is important to take steps to address them.

2. Addressing Secondary Trauma

There are several strategies that can help to address secondary trauma:

- Self-Care: Self-care is crucial in preventing and addressing secondary trauma. This may include practicing mindfulness, exercise, spending time in nature, or engaging in creative activities. Make time for activities that you enjoy and that help you to relax and recharge.

- Seeking Support: It is important to seek support from colleagues, friends, or a mental health professional who understands the impact of secondary trauma.

Talking to others who have experienced similar experiences can help to build a sense of community and support.

- Setting Boundaries: It can be helpful to set boundaries around work and personal life in order to prevent burnout. This may include limiting the number of clients seen in a day, taking regular breaks throughout the day, and establishing a clear separation between work and home life.

- Practicing Self-Compassion: Practicing self-compassion can help to reduce the impact of secondary trauma. This may include speaking kindly to yourself, acknowledging your own limitations and needs, and allowing yourself time to rest and recover.

- Continued Education: Continued education and training on trauma and its effects can help professionals to better understand and address secondary trauma.

Conclusion

Recognizing and addressing secondary trauma is crucial in

preventing burnout and promoting overall well-being for those who work with or care for individuals who have experienced trauma. It is important to prioritize self-care, seek support, set boundaries, practice self-compassion, and continue education and training. By taking these steps, professionals and loved ones can better support themselves and those who have experienced trauma.

27 - Trauma in Children: How to Help and Support

Trauma is an experience that can impact anyone at any point in their lives. However, when children experience trauma, the effects can be especially devastating. Trauma in children can lead to long-lasting emotional, behavioral, and psychological difficulties that can continue into adulthood if not properly addressed. It is essential to understand how to help and support children who have experienced trauma to mitigate the impact of the traumatic event.

What is Trauma in Children?

Trauma in children refers to any experience that overwhelms a child's ability to cope with and process the event emotionally and psychologically. Traumatic events can include natural disasters, abuse, neglect, death of a loved one, accidents, and witnessing or experiencing violence. Trauma can lead to feelings of fear, helplessness, and distress, and it can cause a range of physical, emotional, and behavioral symptoms.

Symptoms of Trauma in Children

The symptoms of trauma in children can vary widely depending on the nature of the traumatic event and the child's age, personality, and coping mechanisms. Some common symptoms of trauma in children include:

1. Emotional Symptoms: Children may become anxious, fearful, irritable, and emotionally unstable after experiencing trauma. They may also feel sad, depressed, or hopeless.

2. Behavioral Symptoms: Children who have experienced trauma may exhibit changes in their behavior, such as withdrawing from friends and family, becoming aggressive, or acting out.

3. Physical Symptoms: Children may experience physical symptoms, such as stomach aches, headaches, sleep disturbances, and other physical complaints.

4. Cognitive Symptoms: Children who have experienced trauma may have difficulty focusing, paying attention, and remembering things. They may also struggle with academic performance.

5. Social Symptoms: Children who have experienced trauma may struggle with social interactions, finding it hard to make friends and to trust others.

How to Help and Support Children who have Experienced Trauma

1. Provide a Safe and Stable Environment: It is essential to provide a stable and secure environment for children who have experienced trauma. This can involve ensuring that basic needs such as food, shelter, and clothing are met, but it also means providing a safe and supportive emotional environment where the child feels safe and can trust those around them.

2. Offer Emotional Support: Children who have experienced trauma need emotional support and encouragement from those around them. Listen to the child's feelings, and validate their emotions. Encourage them to express themselves in healthy ways, such as through drawing, writing, or playing.

3. Get Professional Help: Children who have experienced trauma often require professional help from

mental health professionals who specialize in trauma. Counseling and therapy can be beneficial for children to address and process their emotions and build coping mechanisms.

4. Create a Routine: Trauma can disrupt a child's sense of safety and stability. Creating a routine and structure can help them regain a sense of control over their lives. This can include establishing regular sleep, meal, and study times.

5. Practice Self-care: It is essential to practice self-care as a caregiver when supporting children who have experienced trauma. Taking care of oneself can prevent caregiver burnout and provide the emotional capacity to support the child's needs effectively.

Conclusion

Trauma in children is a severe issue that requires sensitive and careful handling. It is essential to provide a safe and supportive environment for the child, offer emotional support, seek professional help, create a routine, and practice self-care as a caregiver. With appropriate support and interventions, children who have experienced trauma can heal and move forward in their lives.

28 - Trauma in the Workplace: Tips for Employers and Employees

Trauma can impact individuals in all aspects of their lives, including their work. Trauma in the workplace can be caused by a variety of events, such as violence, accidents, harassment, or natural disasters. Trauma can lead to significant emotional and psychological distress that can impact an individual's ability to function in their job. It is essential for employers and employees to understand how to support and address trauma in the workplace effectively.

What is Trauma in the Workplace?

Trauma in the workplace refers to any event that causes physical or emotional harm to an employee. Trauma in the workplace can include incidents such as workplace violence, accidents, natural disasters, harassment, discrimination, or witnessing or experiencing traumatic events on the job. Trauma in the workplace can lead to long-term emotional and psychological effects, impacting an individual's ability to perform their job effectively.

Symptoms of Trauma in the Workplace

28 - TRAUMA IN THE WORKPLACE: TIPS FOR EMPLOYERS AND EMPLOYEES

The symptoms of trauma in the workplace can vary widely depending on the nature of the traumatic event and the individual's coping mechanisms. Some common symptoms of trauma in the workplace include:

1. Emotional Symptoms: Employees may experience feelings of anxiety, depression, fear, anger, or irritability after experiencing trauma in the workplace.

2. Physical Symptoms: Trauma in the workplace can lead to physical symptoms such as headaches, muscle tension, sleep disturbances, or other physical complaints.

3. Cognitive Symptoms: Employees who have experienced trauma in the workplace may have difficulty concentrating, making decisions, or remembering details of their job.

4. Behavioral Symptoms: Trauma in the workplace can lead to changes in an employee's behavior, such as withdrawing from colleagues or work, increased absenteeism, or decreased productivity.

Tips for Employers to Support Employees with Trauma

1. Provide a Safe and Supportive Work Environment: Employers should prioritize creating a safe and supportive work environment for employees who have experienced trauma. This can involve providing a supportive emotional environment and ensuring that basic needs such as food, water, and rest are met.

2. Offer Trauma-Informed Training: Employers can provide trauma-informed training to their employees to help them understand the impact of trauma on their colleagues and how to support them effectively.

3. Provide Resources: Employers should provide employees with access to resources such as employee assistance programs, counseling services, and other mental health resources.

4. Implement Policies and Procedures: Employers can implement policies and procedures that address trauma in the workplace, such as creating a protocol for responding to traumatic events or offering flexible work arrangements for employees who require addi-

tional support.

Tips for Employees to Manage Trauma in the Workplace

1. Practice Self-Care: Employees should prioritize self-care to manage the effects of trauma in the workplace. This can involve taking breaks, engaging in physical activity, and practicing relaxation techniques.

2. Seek Support: Employees should seek support from their colleagues, friends, family, or mental health professionals to process their emotions and manage their symptoms.

3. Communicate with Employers: Employees should communicate with their employers about their needs and how they can be supported. This can involve requesting flexible work arrangements or additional support from colleagues.

4. Take Time Off: Employees may require time off work to process their emotions and manage their symp-

toms. Taking time off can allow employees to prioritize their mental health and well-being.

Conclusion

Trauma in the workplace can be a challenging issue for both employers and employees. Employers can support their employees by providing a safe and supportive work environment, offering trauma-informed training, providing resources, and implementing policies and procedures that address trauma in the workplace. Employees can manage trauma in the workplace by practicing self-care, seeking support, communicating with their employers, and taking time off when necessary. By prioritizing support and addressing trauma

29 - Trauma and Addiction: Breaking the Cycle

Trauma and addiction are closely intertwined, and individuals who have experienced trauma are more likely to develop addiction issues. Trauma can lead to emotional pain and distress, and many people turn to substances as a way to cope with these feelings. Unfortunately, substance abuse can exacerbate trauma symptoms and create a cycle of addiction that is difficult to break. In this chapter, we will explore the relationship between trauma and addiction and discuss ways to break the cycle.

The Relationship Between Trauma and Addiction

Trauma can be defined as any experience that overwhelms an individual's ability to cope and leaves them feeling helpless, frightened, or overwhelmed. Traumatic experiences can include physical or sexual abuse, neglect, domestic violence, natural disasters, or war. Trauma can lead to a variety of mental health issues, including anxiety, depression, and post-traumatic stress disorder (PTSD).

Addiction is characterized by compulsive drug-seeking behavior and drug use despite negative consequences. Addiction can be caused by a variety of factors, including genetics, environmental factors, and trauma. Individuals who have experienced trauma are more likely to develop addiction issues, and addiction can exacerbate trauma symptoms, creating a cycle of addiction and trauma.

Breaking the Cycle of Trauma and Addiction

1. Seek Professional Help: The first step in breaking the cycle of trauma and addiction is to seek professional help. A qualified therapist can help individuals address trauma symptoms and develop healthy coping mechanisms.

2. Address Underlying Trauma: Addressing the underlying trauma is crucial in breaking the cycle of addiction and trauma. Therapy can help individuals process their traumatic experiences and learn healthy ways to cope with their emotions.

3. Practice Self-Care: Practicing self-care is essential in managing trauma and addiction. This can include exercise, mindfulness, and other healthy activities that help reduce stress and promote relaxation.

4. Join Support Groups: Joining support groups can be helpful in breaking the cycle of trauma and addiction. Support groups provide individuals with a safe and supportive environment to share their experiences and receive encouragement and advice from others who have experienced similar struggles.

5. Develop a Strong Support System: Developing a strong support system is crucial in breaking the cycle of trauma and addiction. This can include family, friends, and other supportive individuals who can provide encouragement, accountability, and emotional support.

6. Consider Medication-Assisted Treatment: Medication-assisted treatment can be helpful in breaking the cycle of addiction and trauma. Medications such as methadone, buprenorphine, and naltrexone can help individuals manage cravings and reduce the risk of relapse.

Conclusion

Trauma and addiction are closely intertwined, and breaking

the cycle can be challenging. Seeking professional help, addressing underlying trauma, practicing self-care, joining support groups, developing a strong support system, and considering medication-assisted treatment can all be helpful in breaking the cycle of trauma and addiction. It is essential to remember that recovery is a journey, and it is okay to seek help and support along the way. By addressing the underlying trauma and developing healthy coping mechanisms, individuals can break the cycle of addiction and trauma and lead fulfilling, healthy lives.

30 - Trauma and the Criminal Justice System

Trauma can have a profound impact on individuals who have experienced it, and for some, it can lead to involvement with the criminal justice system. The criminal justice system can be overwhelming and triggering for those who have experienced trauma, and it is important to understand the impact trauma can have on individuals in this context. In this chapter, we will explore trauma and the criminal justice system and discuss ways to support individuals who have experienced trauma in this context.

The Impact of Trauma in the Criminal Justice System

Trauma can have a significant impact on individuals involved in the criminal justice system. For some, trauma may be a contributing factor in their involvement in criminal activity. For others, involvement in the criminal justice system can exacerbate trauma symptoms and lead to further trauma.

Individuals who have experienced trauma may find the criminal justice system overwhelming and triggering. The process of being arrested, detained, and processed through the criminal justice system can be traumatic in and of itself. Additionally, individuals who have experienced trauma may be more likely to experience violence or abuse while in custody or during interactions with law enforcement.

Supporting Individuals with Trauma in the Criminal Justice System

1. Trauma-Informed Care: Trauma-informed care is an approach that recognizes the impact of trauma on individuals and provides services that are sensitive to their needs. This approach involves creating a safe and supportive environment, building trust, and providing care that is non-judgmental and respectful.

2. Advocacy: Advocacy is an essential component of supporting individuals with trauma in the criminal justice system. Advocates can help individuals understand their rights and navigate the legal system, as well as provide emotional support and guidance.

3. Counseling and Therapy: Counseling and therapy can be helpful in addressing trauma symptoms and providing individuals with coping mechanisms to

manage their emotions.

4. Support Groups: Support groups provide individuals with a safe and supportive environment to share their experiences and receive encouragement and advice from others who have experienced similar struggles.

5. Alternative Sentencing: Alternative sentencing programs can be helpful in addressing the underlying issues that may have contributed to an individual's involvement in criminal activity. These programs may include drug treatment, mental health treatment, or community service.

Conclusion

Trauma can have a significant impact on individuals involved in the criminal justice system. The criminal justice system can be overwhelming and triggering for those who have experienced trauma, and it is essential to provide support and care that is sensitive to their needs. Trauma-informed care, advocacy, counseling and therapy, support groups, and alternative sentencing programs can all be helpful in supporting individuals with trauma in the criminal justice system. By providing individuals with the support they need, we can help them overcome trauma and lead fulfilling, healthy lives.

31 - Moving Forward: Creating a New Narrative and Embracing Life

Trauma can be a life-altering experience, but it doesn't have to define who we are or limit our potential for happiness and fulfillment. Moving forward after trauma requires courage, resilience, and a willingness to create a new narrative for our lives. In this chapter, we will explore how to move forward after trauma and embrace life in a new and positive way.

Creating a New Narrative

Trauma can leave us feeling stuck in a negative narrative, but it is possible to rewrite our story and create a new narrative for our lives. Here are some steps to help you create a new narrative:

1. Acknowledge the trauma: Acknowledge what happened and how it has affected you. This can be difficult, but it is an essential step in moving forward.

2. Reframe the narrative: Reframe your story in a more positive light. Instead of focusing on the negative, focus on the positive aspects of your experience, such

as the resilience you have shown or the lessons you have learned.

3. Embrace your strengths: Identify your strengths and focus on them. This can help you build confidence and resilience.

4. Practice self-compassion: Be kind to yourself and practice self-compassion. You deserve love and compassion, especially after what you have been through.

5. Create a vision for your future: Create a vision for your future and focus on your goals. This can help you stay motivated and focused on the positive.

Embracing Life

After experiencing trauma, it can be challenging to embrace life fully. Here are some steps to help you embrace life and move forward:

1. Practice mindfulness: Mindfulness can help you stay present and focused on the positive aspects of your

life.

2. Engage in self-care: Engage in self-care activities that bring you joy and help you feel more connected to yourself.

3. Cultivate positive relationships: Surround yourself with people who uplift and support you.

4. Try new things: Challenge yourself to try new things and explore new experiences. This can help you build confidence and discover new passions.

5. Give back: Giving back to others can be a powerful way to find purpose and meaning in your life.

Conclusion

Moving forward after trauma requires a willingness to create a new narrative for our lives and embrace life in a new and positive way. By acknowledging the trauma, reframing the narrative, embracing our strengths, practicing self-compassion, and creating a vision for our future, we can create a new narrative for our lives. Embracing life requires practicing mindfulness, engaging in self-care, cultivating positive relationships, trying new things, and giving back. By taking these steps, we can overcome trauma and lead fulfilling, meaningful lives.

Thank You

As we come to the conclusion of this book, I would like to express my gratitude for taking the time to read it. It is my aim to spread this information to as many individuals as possible. If you found this book beneficial, I would be extremely grateful if you could leave me a review. This will aid in the book's discoverability by others.

Disclaimer

The purpose of this document is to offer accurate and dependable information on the covered topic and issue. The publication is sold with the understanding that the publisher is not obligated to provide any official, authorized, or professional services. If specialized advice is required, such as legal, financial, medical, or other professional advice, it should be sought from a qualified practitioner.

Please note that this information is not presented by a financial or medical practitioner and is intended for educational, informational, and entertainment purposes only. The content is not meant to replace professional medical advice, diagnosis, or treatment. Always consult with your physician or another qualified healthcare provider for any medical condition you may have. Do not disregard professional medical advice or delay in seeking it because of something you read in this document.

The information provided here is believed to be accurate and consistent. However, any liability resulting from any usage or abuse of any policies, processes, or directions contained herein is the sole responsibility of the reader. Under no circumstances will the publisher be held responsible for

DISCLAIMER

any damages, losses, or monetary losses resulting from the information in this document, whether directly or indirectly.